German Proverbs

St. John the Evangelist

Ein Buch ist wie ein Garten, den man in der Tasche trägt.

A book is like a garden that you can put in your pocket.

German Proverbs

Collected by Julie McDonald,
Lynn Hattery-Beyer, and
Joan Liffring-Zug

Edited by John Zug

Calligraphy by Esther Feske

Bauernmalerei folk art cover
by Helen Elizabeth Blanck

Woodcuts from
The Nuremberg Chronicle,
1493

Part of the "Lineage of Christ"

ISBN 0-9717025-3-5

Copyright © 1988 Penfield
Library of Congress #87-63365

For a list of all titles, write:
Penfield Books
215 Brown Street
Iowa City, IA 52245-1358

Acknowledgments

A special thank you to Marlene Domeier, New Ulm, Minnesota; Lanny Haldy and Barbara Hoehnle, Museum of Amana History, Amana, Iowa; Virginia Myers, Professor of Art, and Harry Oster, Professor of English and Folklore, University of Iowa; Gustave and Fran von Groschwitz, New York, N.Y.; Judy Sutcliffe, Santa Barbara, California; Gladys Benz and Dorothy Crum of Iowa City; and Kathryn Chadima, Cedar Rapids, Iowa.

Illustrations in German Proverbs are by Wolgemut and Pleydenwuff, artists who lived in Germany in the late 1400's. They obtained superb reproductions by cutting away wood so that what remained of the surface of the woodblock could be inked and then reproduced on paper. These woodcuts were used in the beautiful Nuremberg Chronicle (1493), which ranks with the Gutenberg Bible as one of the first and finest achievements after Johannes Gutenberg's invention of movable type made the printed word available to the people. The painter-like quality of the illustrations led to the belief that the great German artist Albrecht Dürer (1471-1528) was responsible for many of the woodcuts. Dürer was born in Nuremberg and was working in Wolgemut's studio at the time the book was in preparation. Over 600 individual woodcuts were made, many being used several times to represent different historical figures or great cities, so some 2,000 illustrations can be counted.

The Nuremberg Chronicle proclaimed itself "the book of chronicles and stories with characters and pictures from the beginning of the world to our time." Blank pages were provided on which the owner could add new developments, (people hadn't yet heard of Columbus's discovery of the New World, but they did assume the Earth was round). Each Chronicle originally sold for three Rheinish guilders, about one-fiftieth the cost of a large house.

Calligraphy in German Proverbs is based on the type in the Chronicle—a formal "Black Letter" for German text and headlines, and this rounder, transitional style for the English. We hope this contributes to your sense of the culture as you savor these proverbs.

Just like German fairy tales, German proverbs are often phrased as moral lessons, reminders of the values important in the culture. A German proverb often says more than a thick book or a long lecture. German proverbs have always been philosophical, catechisms for everyday life.   -Lynn Hattery-Beyer

To hear the lullaby that leads to Grand Opera, the prudent advice that leads to strategy, the apt observation that leads to great literature and philosophy, and the murmur of the heart that leads to ringing theology, consider the proverbs of the German people. The short, wise sayings handed down from generation to generation have been forged by centuries of common experience. They come from the gemütlich (comfortable, at ease) moments of life that we all know and cherish.   -Julie McDonald

Olimpias alex
anders muter

Nectabanus
alexâders vater

Love and Marriage

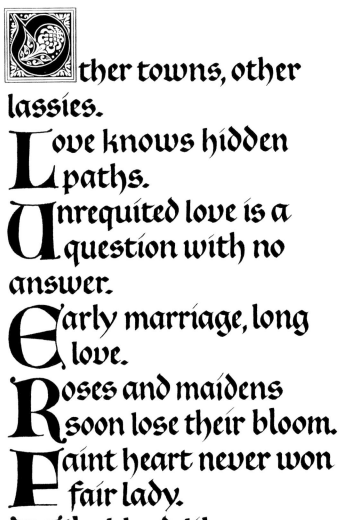

Other towns, other lassies.

Love knows hidden paths.

Unrequited love is a question with no answer.

Early marriage, long love.

Roses and maidens soon lose their bloom.

Faint heart never won fair lady.

Like blood, like means, and like age make the happiest marriage.

Coffee and love are best when they're hot.

The beginning hot, the middle lukewarm, the end cold.

Beauty is a good letter of introduction.

He who has the fortune brings home the bride.

The Ark of Noah

Saving is a greater art than gaining.

The best friends are in one's purse.

Tomorrow, tomorrow, not today, all the lazy people say.

When a man is rich he begins to save.

It usually rains where it's already wet.

For the diligent, a week has seven days; for the slothful, seven tomorrows.

Arbeitsamkeit ist die beste Lotterie.

Industriousness is the best lottery.

Regensburg, Bavaria

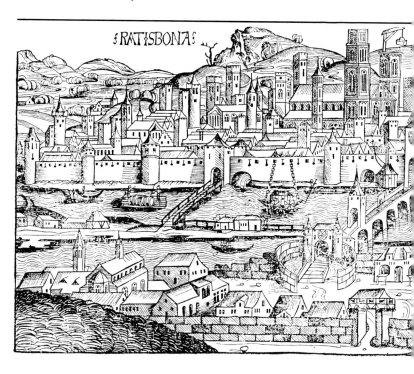

Wer die Arbeit erfunden
hat, der muß nichts zu
tun gehabt haben.

Whoever invented work
must not have had
anything to do.

War is pleasant for those who have not tried it.

Better an unjust peace than a just war.

When God means to punish a nation, he deprives the rulers of wisdom.

Who bows to might loses his right.

It's better to have an egg in times of peace than a hen during war.

War is like a lottery — you never know who will win.

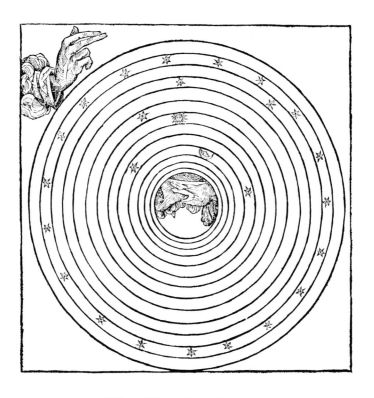

The Hand of God,
The Fourth Day of Creation

If you put out another's candle, you also will be in the dark.

Nobody is trodden upon unless he lies down first.

Clean your plate and tomorrow will be a nice day.

He who is grateful for a kindness unlocks the door for another.

Be not ashamed of your craft.

Never give advice unasked.

The Fifth Day of Creation

Advising is easier than helping.

When you sweep the stairs, you start at the top.

Never trust to another what you should do yourself.

Don't try to fly before you've grown feathers.

Praise the mountains and stay in the valley.

Diligent weeding is better than praying.

Creation of the hosts of heaven

The best penitence:
never do it again.

A hundred years of regret pays not a farthing of debt.

Set a thief to catch a thief.

If you don't light fires, smoke won't get in your eyes.

Thue Recht und
Scheue Niemand.
Do right and shun
no one.

Speaking comes by nature, silence by understanding.

Be silent, or say something better than silence.

Talking is silver, silence is gold.

No one betrays himself by silence.

Silence is a fence around wisdom.

Creation of Eve

Adam must have an Eve to blame for his own faults.

Nothing dries sooner than tears.

A poor person isn't he who has little, but he who needs a lot.

The wiser person yields, but the donkey doesn't, and falls into the brook.

What three know will soon be known to thirty.

A fence lasts three years, a dog lasts three fences, a horse lasts three dogs, and a man lasts three horses.

He who thinks of death begins to live.

The morning hour has gold in its mouth.

Green Christmas, white Easter.

Bad times make good men.

Learned fools exceed all fools.

Forgiven is not forgotten.

Moses receives the Ten Commandments

As fast as laws are devised, their evasion is contrived.

Argument is a sieve for sifting truth.

Each one knows best where his own shoe pinches.

Many who build castles in the air cannot build a hut on earth.

What is sport to the cat is death to the mouse.

Little folks are fond of talking about what great folks do.

Lini der der Richter

Linea
Iolue
Judicñ

Othoniel

Aioth

Sangar

Wine upon beer is very good cheer; beer upon wine consider with fear.

To good eating belongs good drinking.

The fish lead a pleasant life; they drink when they like.

Thousands drink themselves to death before one dies of thirst.

There are more old tipplers than old doctors.

Everything has an end, but a sausage has two.

In water you may see your own face, in wine the heart of another.

No one is luckier than he who thinks he's in luck.

No answer really is an answer.

He who deals in onions no longer smells them.

Not every ass has long ears.

At a round table, every seat is the head place.

Joy and sorrow are today and tomorrow.

Were there no fools, there would be no wise men.

'Tis the mind ennobles, not the blood.

A good word costs nothing.
The sundial counts only the bright hours.

Happy is the one who forgets that which cannot be changed.

Mirth is the sugar of life.

A day without laughter is a day lost.

Misfortunes have their good sides, too.

A penny's worth of cheerfulness can dispel a pound of problems.

Those who can be happy today should not wait until tomorrow.

Fröhlich Gemüt gibt gesundes Blut.

A cheerful disposition breeds healthy heirs.

Trier, Germany, was founded by Romans. This woodcut was reused as "Metz", which is now French.

Anstatt zu klagen, daß
die Rosen Dornen haben,
Freude solltest du haben,
daß der Dornstrauch
Rosen trägt.

Instead of complaining
that the rosebush is full
of thorns, be happy
that the thornbush has
roses.

We hang minor thieves and tip our hats to major ones.

Revenge is a meal that must be eaten cold.

Death is the poor man's doctor.

He who believes easily is easily deceived.

Sweet song has betrayed many.

Remorse is lust's dessert.

Sweet wine makes sour vinegar.

Iß, trink, sei fröhlich hier auf Erd', denk nur nicht, daß es besser werd.

Eat, drink and be merry here on earth - just don't think that things will get better.

"A gruesome pestilence"

Dreams are froth.
The world is a Turkish
bath. The higher you
sit, the more you sweat.
Ambition and fleas
both jump high.
The higher a monkey
climbs, the more he
shows his behind.
Experience is a long
road and an expensive
school.
If the eye does not want
to see, neither light nor
glasses will help.
Better to be one-eyed
than blind.

Friends and Neighbors

If you want to know yourself, offend two or three of your neighbors.

Love your neighbor, but don't pull down the fence.

One foe is too many and a hundred friends are too few.

Wish for neither fools nor saints as neighbors.

Real friendship does not freeze in winter.

Presents keep friendships warm.

Wer einen guten Freund hat, braucht keinen Spiegel.

If you have a good friend, you don't need a mirror.

Ulm, Germany

Ehrlicher Feind ist besser als falscher Freund.

Better an honest enemy than a false friend.

Straßburg

Honesty

Truth gives a short answer; lies go round about. Every lie needs to be fed ten more. Truth is medicine which must be given at the right time.

Wenn die Katz eine Henne wäre, leget' sie Eier.

If the cat were a chicken, she'd lay eggs.

Learning

It's not healthy to swallow books without chewing.

Those who get lost on the way to school will never find their way through life.

An uneducated person is like an unpolished mirror.

He who teaches children learns more than they do.

The tree must be bent while it is young.

The Young and The Old

Every mother's child
is handsome.

The small child
tramples on mother's
skirt, the older child on
her heart.

To remain young while
growing old is the
highest blessing.

The oldest trees often
bear the sweetest
fruit.

Time is a robber and a
thief, stealing youth
and love.

Young men with Coats of Arms

He who wants to warm himself in old age must build a fireplace in his youth.

Age writes in sand, youth in stone.

He who teaches a boy teaches three: a youth, a young man, and an old man.

Those who don't pick roses in summer won't pick them in winter either.

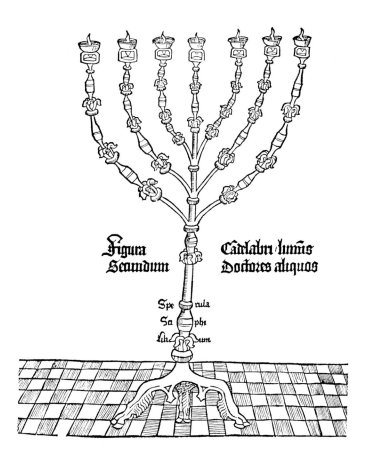

Figura
Secundum

Cãdlabri lumis
Doctores aliquos

Spe rula
Sa phi
lib um

A Higher Power

Fear has created more gods than piety.

God blesses the seeking rather than the finding.

God gives, but man must open his hand.

When need is greatest, God is nearest.

Those who love in the Lord never see each other for the last time.

God favors the one who gives to the poor.

Monastery Schadentall

Doctor Luther's shoes
do not fit every
parish priest.
Those who are too pious
want to enter heaven
with their shoes and
stockings on.
The fewer the words,
the better the prayer.
Every man for himself,
and God for us all.

Burning the Library
at Alexandria

Sprichwörter sind wie Schmetterlinge, einige werden gefangen, andere fliegen davon.

Proverbs are like butterflies; some are caught and some fly away.

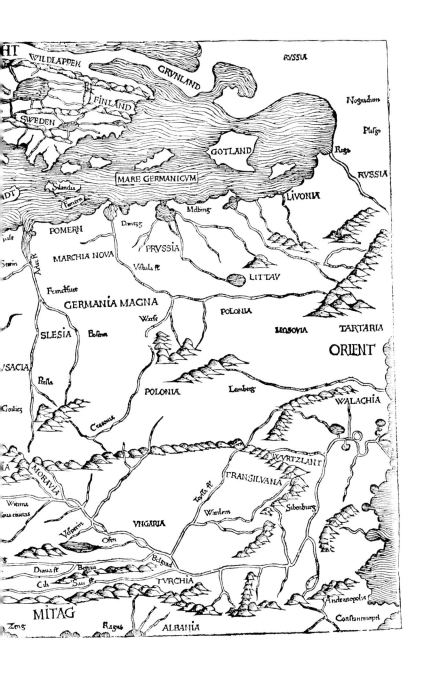